Meet Spike

Let's Learn About Epilepsy

Spike and the Gang Series: Book 1

By: Leslie Pedreira, APRN

This Book Series is dedicated to all the amazing patients I have had the privilege of caring for through the years! Your courage and strength inspired me to write these books!

Hi! My name is Spike. Most people who meet me call me trouble. I travel most of the time, but sometimes I find a place that makes me happy.

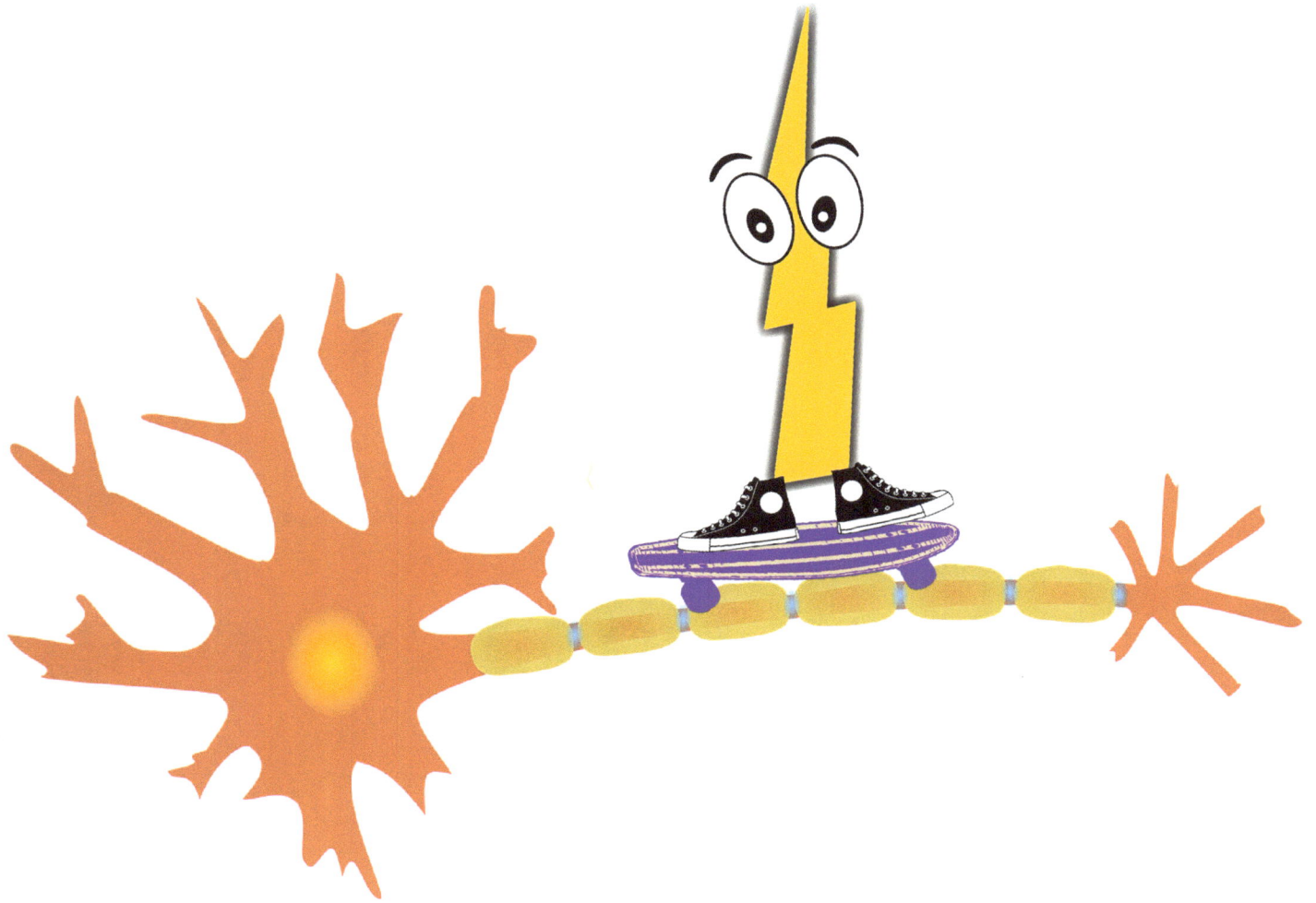

Sometimes I travel alone. Sometimes my friend Sharpie and my cousin Polly come along. No one likes us hanging out together as we do not like to sleep.

We know we are trouble makers, but we just can't stop having fun!

DON'T STOP THE PARTY!

So why does everyone say we are so bad? Well...this is a very tough question to answer in a simple way.

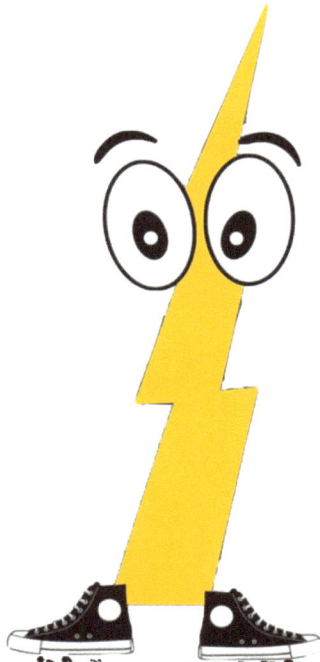

People do not want us around because we can cause a seizure (seez-yure). Some people call seizures spells, events, fits or attacks.

They can be scary to watch.

A seizure can happen when Sharpie, Polly or I feel like changing the activity of your brain. It can be like lightning when it storms. We think it is funny, but no one else does.

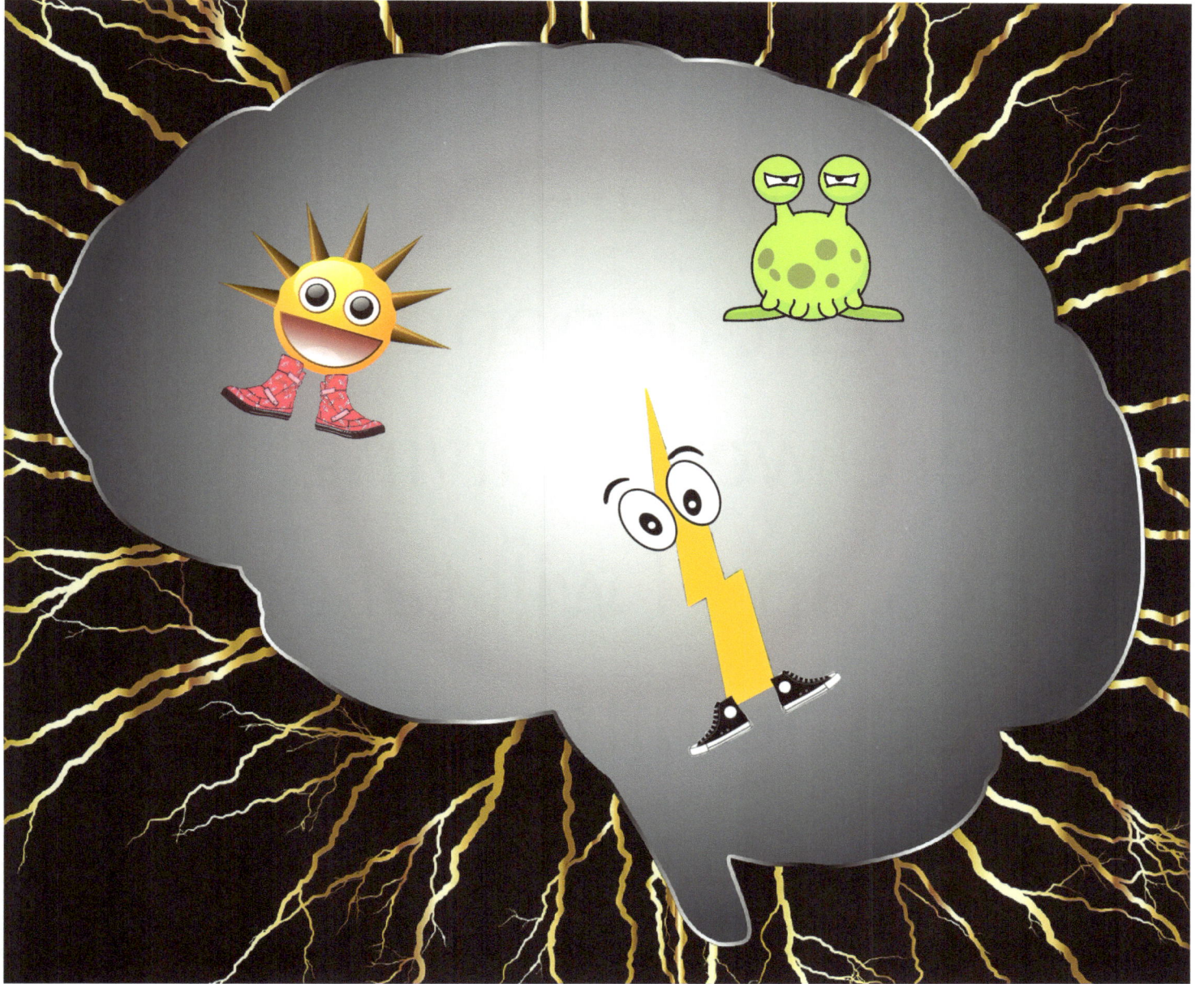

Your brain has different parts and each part has a job. A seizure can look different depending on where we are living. My friends and I will talk more about the different parts of your brain later on.

There can be reasons why we come to stay. None of those reasons are your fault. Most of the time, no one knows why we move in. They call that idiopathic (id-io-path-ic) epilepsy (ep-uh-lep-sy). Sometimes we can even hide for a while before we are found!

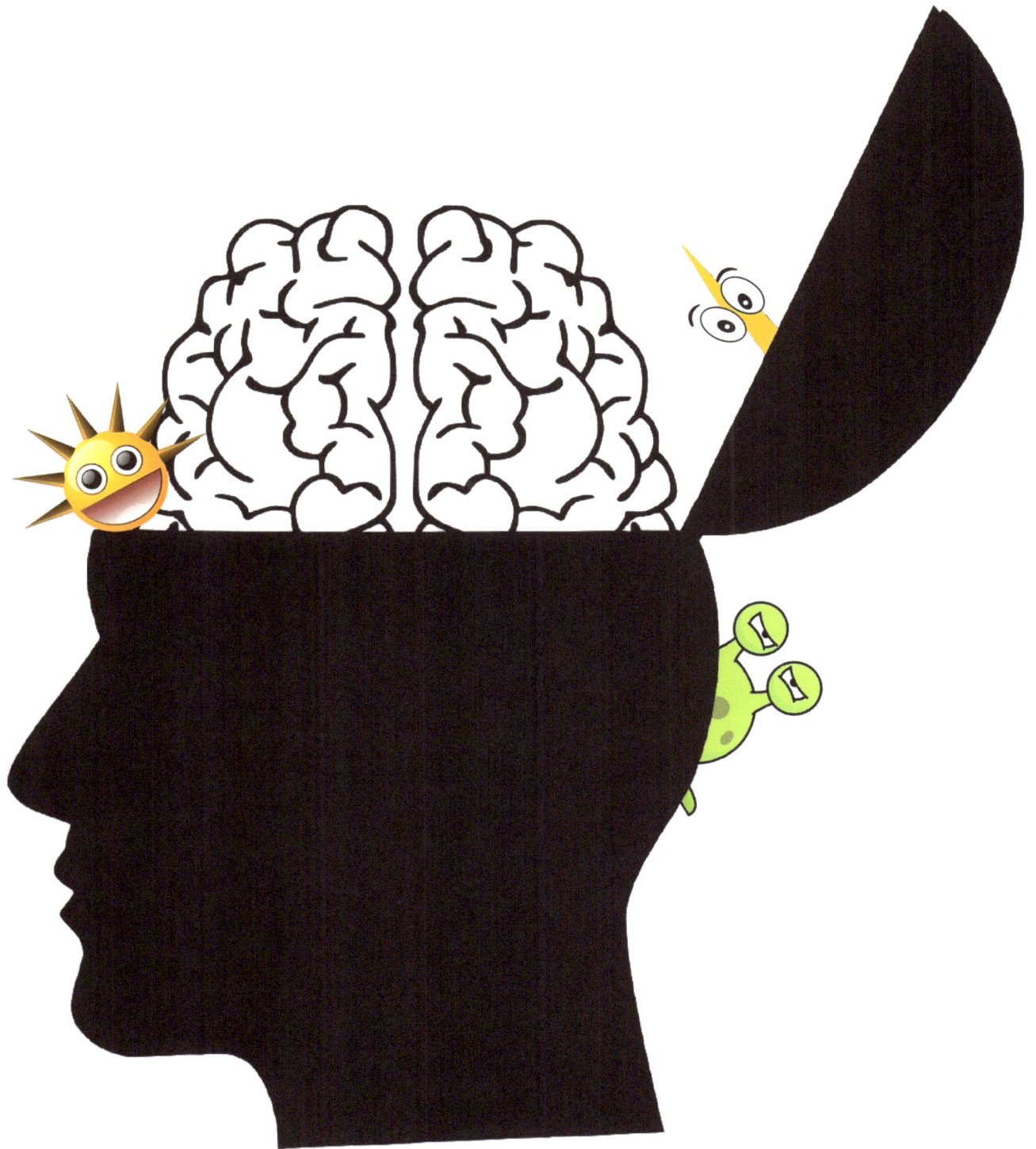

We can cause all kinds of trouble even when we don't make a seizure.

sleep changes

learning problems

behavior changes

developmental changes

headaches

attention issues

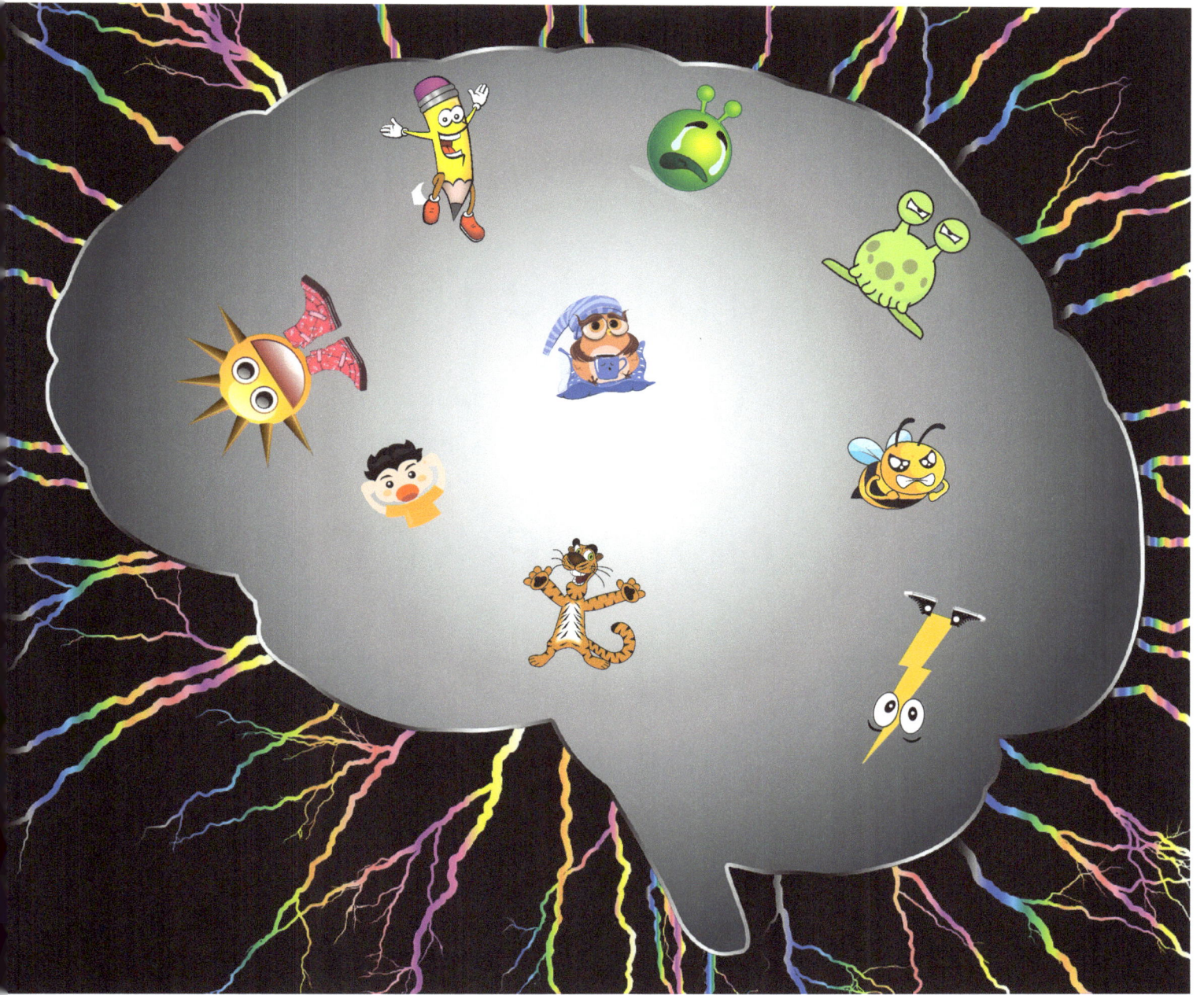

We have an enemy. His name is Super Med. We do not like him. He makes us unhappy. When he knocks on our door we know we may have to move soon.

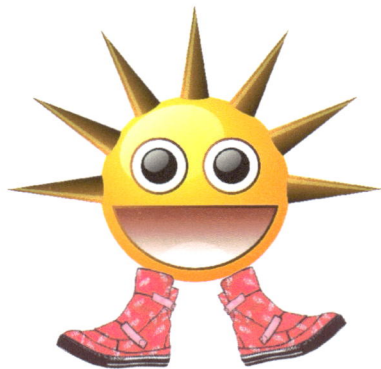

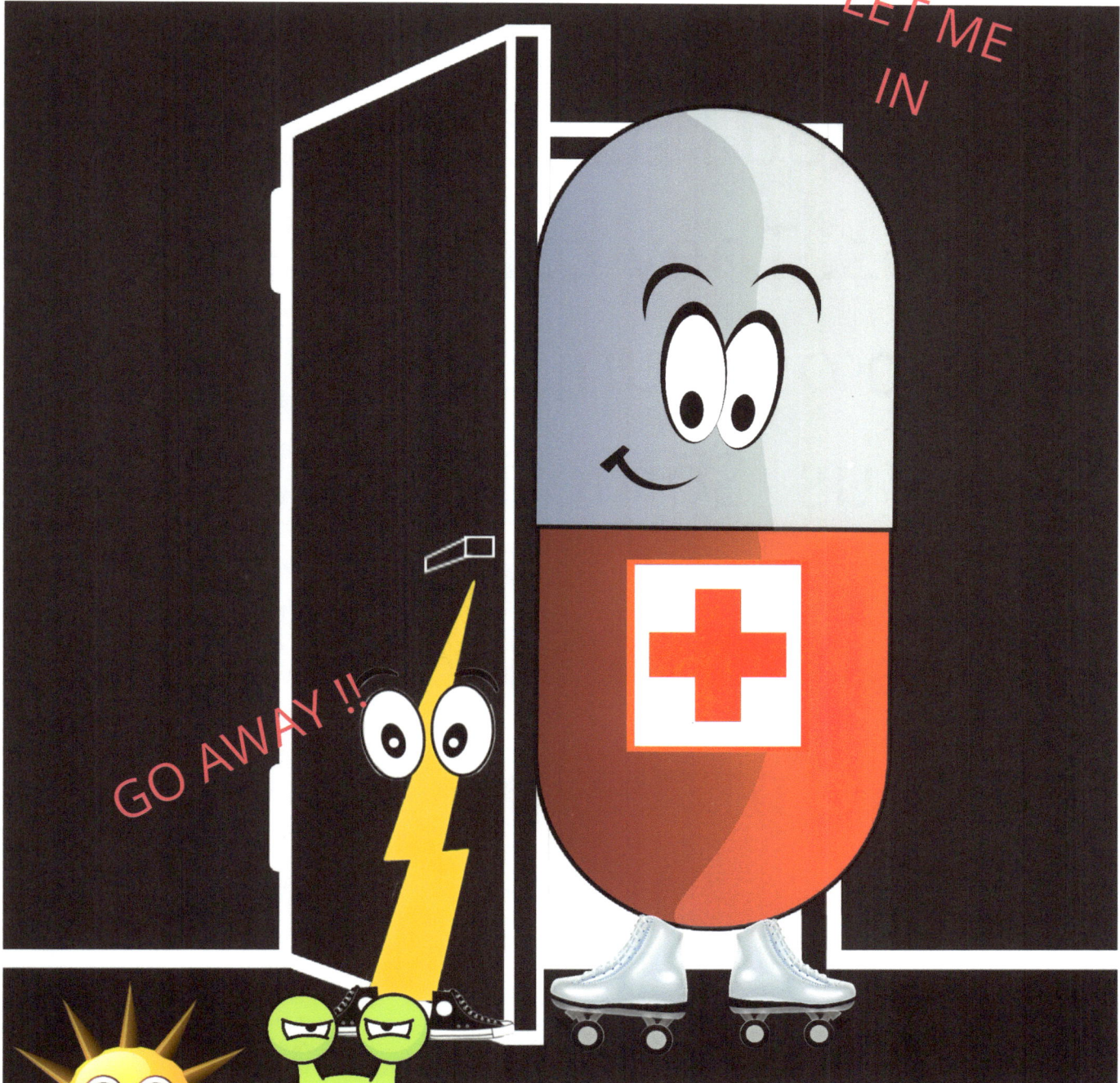

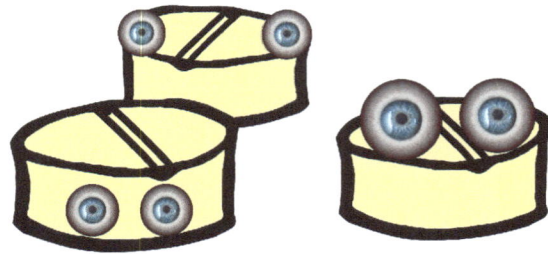

Super Med has his own gang of friends. They come in and try to stop our fun. Sometimes he beats us. Sometimes we win.

Today Super Med won. We have to move, but we will be back!!

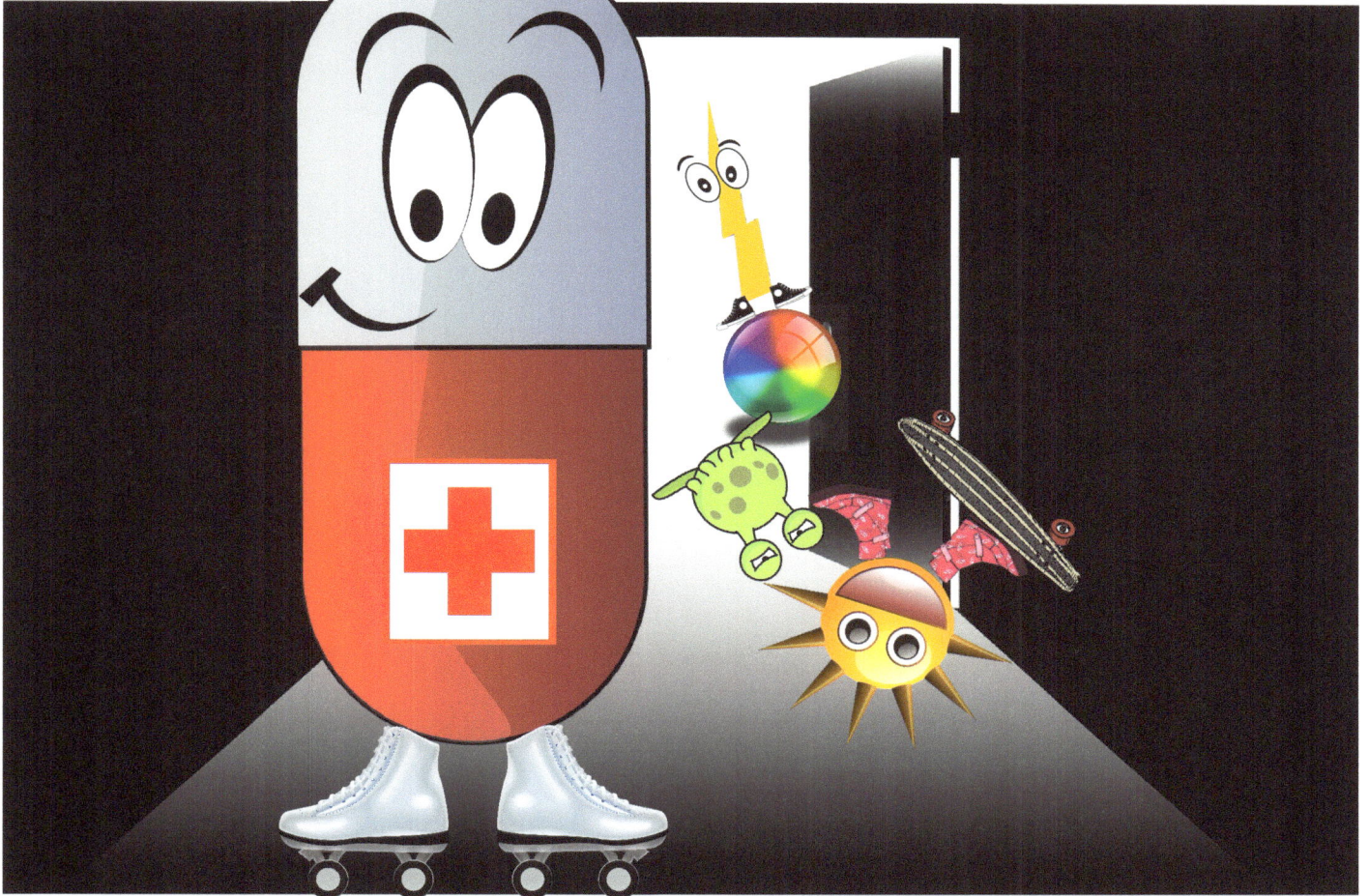